D1608758

Good Manners
in Relationships

Good Manners
with Your Siblings

by Rebecca Felix
illustrated by Gary LaCoste

magic
wagon

visit us at www.abdopublishing.com

Published by Magic Wagon, a division of the ABDO Group, PO Box 398166, Minneapolis, MN, 55439.

Looking Glass Library™ is a trademark and logo of Magic Wagon.

Printed in the United States of America, North Mankato, Minnesota.
102013
012014

 The book contains at least 10% recycled materials.

Text by Rebecca Felix
Illustrations by Gary LaCoste
Edited by Stephanie Hedlund and Rochelle Baltzer
Interior layout and design by Renée LaViolette
Cover design by Renée LaViolette

Library of Congress Cataloging-in-Publication Data

Felix, Rebecca, 1984-
  Good manners with your siblings / by Rebecca Felix ; illustrated by Gary LaCoste.
     pages cm. -- (Good manners in relationships)
  Includes index.
  Audience: Age 3-10.
  ISBN 978-1-62402-027-8
1. Etiquette for children and teenagers--Juvenile literature. 2. Brothers and sisters--Juvenile literature. I. LaCoste, Gary, illustrator. II. Title.
  BJ1857.C5F372 2014
  395.1'22--dc23
                    2013028881

Contents

Why Do Good Manners Matter with Siblings?

Bo is reading his new book. His younger sister, Ava, enters the room. She sits right next to Bo. He sighs. He doesn't like Ava sitting so close. Ava asks to read Bo's book when he is done.

Bo frowns. It is his brand-new book! Ava can't even read all the words yet. And she might wrinkle or rip the pages. What should Bo do?

Bo should share his book with Ava. He should be polite when he answers her. He can ask her to be careful with the book. Then Bo can ask Ava to give him room while he finishes reading.

Brothers and sisters live in the same space. They use many of the same things. Sharing with siblings shows good manners. It also makes it easier to get along.

Boys and girls can enjoy all games and toys. Not sharing because something is "only for" a boy or a girl is not nice.

How would siblings treat each other without good manners? Bo might push Ava away from him. He might say she cannot read his book. Ava might rip the book away from Bo. Both siblings would probably become upset. They might get in trouble for fighting.

Show Good Manners with Siblings!

Respect is the base of good manners. Showing respect means treating others how you like to be treated. It also means treating their things nicely. Treating siblings with respect shows you care about them and their things. What other manners are important with siblings?

Show step siblings the same respect as siblings.

11

Being kind is another base of good manners.
Brothers and sisters spend a lot of time together.
They see each other when they are not at their best.
Siblings might look funny when they wake up. They
might be grumpy when they are sick.

It is never nice to tease a sibling or to be mean
when they make mistakes. Being kind in these
situations shows good manners. It can make sibling
relationships stronger in good and bad times.

Talking politely to siblings is good manners. "Please" should be used to ask for help. This is a "magic word." Ava should ask Bo to please help her with a word while reading. Saying "please" makes a brother or sister more likely to help out.

15

Ava should say the magic words "thank you" after Bo helps her. "Thank you" should also be said when siblings lend you something. It is also the correct reply when they say or do something nice. This shows siblings that their actions or words are appreciated.

The polite response when someone tells you "thank you" is to say "you're welcome."

Bo and Ava are going outside. Bo wants to play Frisbee. Ava wants to play Ping-Pong. Bo does not like playing Ping-Pong. Ava does not like Frisbee. Neither game is fun alone. What should Bo and Ava do?

They should take turns. They can spend time playing both games. This is fair and shows good manners. Taking turns shows siblings that what they want to do matters too.

It is also good manners to take turns doing different chores.

Bo and Ava might decide to play Frisbee first. If they do, Ava's choice should be first next time. This will set them up to use good manners next time they play together. They will already know whose turn it is to pick the first game.

Bo throws the Frisbee too hard. It hits Ava in the head. It was an accident. Two magic words will let Ava know this. Bo should tell Ava "I'm sorry."

"I'm sorry" lets a sibling know you feel bad. It will also help them forgive you. Now get ready to see some good manners in motion!

23

Manners in Motion

Bo and Ava's dad is taking them to the movies. At the car, Ava asks, "Bo, can I please ride in front?"

"Sure," Bo says. "We can take turns. I'll ride in front on the way home."

"Thank you!" Ava says.

"You're welcome," Bo says.

Bo and Ava each get to pick out candy for the movie. They both want sour fruit chews. But the movie theater is almost out! They only have one bag left.

"You can have first pick, Ava," Bo says.

"We can share the last bag!" Ava says.

During the movie, Ava feels sick. They have to leave before the movie ends. Bo is upset. But he does not want Ava to feel bad.

"It's okay, Ava. We'll rent the movie later," Bo says. "I hope you feel better."

How did Bo and Ava show each other good manners? Both were polite and kind. Showing siblings good manners is easy! Just remember to treat siblings with respect. What good manners have you practiced with siblings lately?

29

Amazing Facts about Manners with Siblings

What's In a Name

What do you call your siblings? Many people call their siblings by their first name in the United States. Other cultures have different ideas of good manners between siblings. In Japan, younger siblings show older siblings respect by what they call them. They often call them "older brother" or "older sister" instead of their name. Many siblings in Korea do this as well.

Good Manners When Arguing

Did you know that almost all siblings argue? Even with good manners, arguments can happen. It is important to use good manners even when arguing. Never hit your sibling. Don't call them names. It is not good manners to yell. Be kind and show siblings respect, even when you argue.

Top Five Tips for Good Manners with Siblings

1. Be kind.
2. Treat siblings with respect.
3. Share.
4. Take turns.
5. Don't forget to say "please," "thank you," and "excuse me!"

Glossary

appreciate — to recognize and be thankful for something.

chores — jobs or tasks.

lend — to let someone use something that they will return to you.

polite — showing good manners by the way you act or speak.

situation — the event of a certain moment.

Web Sites

To learn more about manners, visit ABDO Group online at **www.abdopublishing.com**. Web sites about manners are featured on our Book Links page. These links are routinely monitored and updated to provide the most current information available.

Index